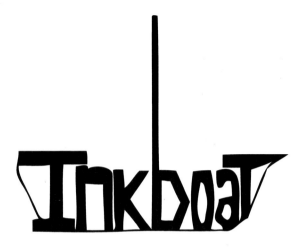

Poems by
Salvatore Salerno

BEFOREWORDS

The poems that I wrote from April 1975 to May 1985 were collected in *Sunleaf*. For twenty-three years after that, I wrote no poetry, only prose. I can't explain the lapse. I wrote the poems in this volume from June 2008 to July 2013. *Inkboat*, as with *Sunleaf*, is dedicated to my beloved Barbara, Christina and Laura, for the fulfillment of my life. I am grateful to the editors of the following publications for printing the following poems:

CHAFFIN JOURNAL: Our Favorite Pastime, Passing Time; Intentions Don't Matter to the Raccoon

THE ECLECTIC MUSE: Achilles Redux; Ars Longa, Vita Brevis Est; After the Footfall

INVERTED A-HORN: Unfinished Business

MORE THAN SOIL, MORE THAN SKY: The Scheherazade Gene

THE NEW YEAR'S POETRY CHALLENGE: The Loss of Jenny Entwhistle; Philomena, with Feeling

POEM: This, at Least; Article of Faith

POST POEMS: Logwise, I'm Sure

SNAIL MAIL REVIEW: The Weir; On a Saunter

STANISLAUS CONNECTIONS: Broken on Fortune's Wheel; Peace, That Holding Action; Close Enough to Christmas Eve; Sad Carnival

THE STORYTELLER: The Widow Quinn

QUERCUS REVIEW: Less is Most

Cover photos by Barbara Gill Salerno
Title Lettering by Brady Howells
For best results, open in sunlight

CONTAINING WITHIN:

ENVOI
(with a pinch from Chaucer)

'Go, litel bok, go,' vessel of words,
And sail this tumultuous world
Through the eyes to waves of mind,
Float from heart to kindred heart—
Then seek harbor on the silent shelf
From the common storm, Oblivion;
Your builder bids you fond farewell
With hope for the time that's lasting,
Ever sought by the fleeting pens
Of all fellow writers passing.

THE RETURN OF SHE WHO RHYMES WITH 'ITCH'

Teach me to be idle!
She must have come by alleyway,
beneath the loose fence boards
and through my open kitchen door
while I was doing nothing well.

Euterpe, ex-mistress and muse,
settled in my chair, crossing
those gorgeous legs, smiling
with those luscious lips, and pointed
a delicate finger at my pen. After
twenty-three years, she hadn't aged one day.

Her look absorbed my gaping stare.
I stammered, "You've got to be. . .
is this a cruel joke? Are you blind?
Don't you see the very face
that scares me in my mirror?
On a good day, I'm a sideways dog;
on a bad, a shuffling stick with clothes.
Go and seduce some lusty man
with time for your passionate teasing
who is willing to sway to your
painful songs with longing."

Silently, she pressed her lyre
closer to her shapely breasts,
shaking her pretty head, tossing
her curls of sun-spun gold
and pointed to my pen again.
 "But...what? But...why...?"
I sputtered like a rusty tap,
"in this, my final season,
my readers pared down to ten;
my star has risen and set;
fame knocked but once and fled,
my fortune of a career is spent!
What earthly good, what purpose...?"

She stopped me with a finger raised,
then replied in a voice that rang
in the tone of a distant bell,
"Don't ask, I have my reasons!"

I looked too long at her charming face,
I looked too deep into her blue eyes,
and knew that I was done.
Lacking the will to evict her
or the wile to disagree,
so here I bend to my futile task,
ungratefully aroused
and blind as a love must be.

INTENTIONS DON'T MATTER TO THE RACCOON

They stared at the dark, glistening road
through a rain falling hard as his grip on the wheel.
"You did it again." She replied with silence.

"You belittled me in front of those people back there."
She folded her hands. "I didn't."
The silence was hard as the road before.

"If so, I didn't intend to."
They saw a blur, felt a thump beneath.
That's when he muttered what he said.

A year later to the day, in a similar rain,
they joined their names to the papers,
which their children have still not forgiven.

SNAKE ON THE ROAD

It needs the warmth of light;
Its blood is cold.
 It should have stopped
   Beside the road.

                   And there an end.

 He could have stopped
   Beside the road.
He needs the light of warmth;
His blood is cold.

UNFINISHED BUSINESS

The gadgets are whirring, they're whirring,
And their whisper is like a low wind,
Your eyelids are heavy, my children,
You're tired, you're falling asleep,
   While the fish and the whales and dolphins
   Are swimming about in the deep.

The boxes are flashing, they're flashing
With pictures we cannot resist—
You're under my spell, my devoted,
Don't worry, you're going nowhere,
  While the hawks and the eagles and ravens
  Are soaring aloft in the air.

The screens are all shining, they're shining
In a language we all understand—
Give me your will, my servants,
Obey what we shall command,
  While the wolves and the deer and cougars
  Are running all over the land.

The rulers of earth are relaxing,
Not plotting their feverish plans,
 Some earth for the moment is resting,
 And healing as best as it can;

Creatures are calling with primitive voices
Their masters cannot understand;
All the birds of the sky, and the fish in the sea,
And the beasts all over the land
Are restless, they're restlessly staying alive
And free in the fragile reprieve.

FOUND AND LOST

My friend gave me a bright compass
before our path diverged, and we
pledged our ways would cross someday,
that loyalty would seek a common way.
Invisible now, he is elsewhere beneath the sun
or conscripted with the legions of dead.

I was on a journey to remember him,
my morning afloat in gold—
every path I stepped was in the right,
every path I shunned was wrong,
my compass tuned to the earth lodestone.

Lonely at midday, I hoped for company
when two men came from another trail.
We drank, laughed and sang a while—
the man in front broke bread for me
while the one at my back turned me all to black.

I rose from a ditch, bleeding and sore,
my wallet gone, the compass smashed for spite.
Dazed in a haze, I lost my trail,
turning, stopping, turning around,
choosing paths that were all dead ends—
turning, wandering, turning again,
I was the center of a trackless wood.
Clouds arrived in tricking shades of gray
that hid the lodestar from my eyes.

My afternoon was encased in lead,
my breath suffused with doubt.
Darkness falling caught me unaware
sooner than I had imagined.
I had provisions enough for night,
though just a cloak for warmth.

I lay with a will among stones,
I stared at a million alien stars
made as cold from their distance
as my near one's warm by rising.

I only had to outlast the night.

I heard an owl give a lovely trill
before pouncing down to kill,
and the murmuring heart of water.

Tomorrow I'll follow that creek down
to roads that lead to comforts—
getting home on unplanned routes
on the loans of strangers' mercies.

I know everything comes with a price.
I could buy another compass there,
yet I cannot trust the marketplace—
only heartfelt gifts stay true.

Tomorrow I'll be found again
and brought to a land of bread and lies
where gifts are easily broken,
where flinty hearts win the day,
and the soft and the weak are losers.

FORTUNATE ARE THOSE

Something never loves success,
so lies in wait at every place--
            no sooner have you begun
to make a monument of yourself,
            stone and mortar on stone,
            than it begins as well:
            first, by moss and lichen
growing in seams; then tendrils
seek holds, burrow in cracks
            separating joints;
            then the rain falls,
pouring into every flaw,
            widening the split,
            crumbling the loose;
            the earth works next,
            devouring, as the sun
follows wind and ice and rain,
            until your hallowed place
reverts to what was there again.

            Fortunate are those
            who have found this
            early in their building,
            so they may cherish
            the motions of their bodies,
            the heft of every stone,
            honor the hands of helpers,
and savor the bread of all shared days
salted with sweat and leavened by pain.

PHARMACEUTOPIA

One pill to awake,
Another for snoring,
A third to keep
From being boring.

A pill for arousal,
Another for relief,
A couple to prevent you
From being a thief.

A drug to enjoy
Getting on the bus,
Another to tolerate
People like us.

Pills for remaining
Clever or lean,
More for surviving
Beyond your means.

My ancestral kin
Hunted and harvested;
Yours did, too.
When they got mad,
Or foolish or sad
How, pray tell,
Did they make do?

Breathing's sweet,
But living's tough,
So shut your face
And suck it up:
All's well that ends—
Well, soon enough.

ROUNDABOUT

The painted horses of this static race
        Stand, each with an axis through its back,
        Connected from blue roof to scruffy floor
As the hustlers grab the outside track,
        Leaving others for the slow
        Who care only to go.

A man with a mask of indifferent face
        Does a thing unseen, and the horses
        Rise and fall to a haunting tune,
Moving us like fate in their stiff courses—
        We on the inside smile,
        If only for a while.

A metal arm in a reachable place
        Dispenses rings of iron and brass
        That the riders, leaning forward—
All in the timing—grab when they pass,
        Shouting their lucky joy
        When they pluck a toy.

The iron can be tossed at a large clown's face
        On the wall, but the brass earns the prize
        Of winning something cheap for free.
I settle for motions of lesser size,
        Grip tight so I won't slide
        Off this crazy ride.

OUR FAVORITE PASTIME, PASSING TIME

For as long as it takes to read these lines, always less than the moments
To lay them down, crystal grains kin to those at the ocean shore, though
Not unnumbered as stars, but meticulously weighed and poured into
Glass bulbs, these grains of no sure harvest obey gravity, thus taking
On *gravitas* when watched by you or me. You've made a choice that
Makes me grateful, having no better time than *now* to engage in play
Though the loud world shouts, even as the level plain has turned to
A hill, and the collapse of the cone on top serves as reminder, as if
We need one, not *tempus fugit* because this ship of sand and wood
And glass does not contain the mystery as much as measures it,
But that time move *through* us, a baffling phenomenon.
An equal amazement is the mind behind our
Eyes that gaze at the glass, true lodestone
For being, and in being the only beings
In what's known so far as
The universe in our
Desire not only
To fall,
Fall
With
Small
Pain and
Less suffering,
What we share with
Beasts, but also to make
Meaning as we go along,
Because the sands now, look,
Appear to try to beat us in a race
Of inanimate zeal to empty out on
Top and fill a mound as if to bury something.
This one page is an apt border to contain a poem
And the bottom of this one is approaching more mass
As words drop onto it, and we have together occupied
A singular point in time and space for just this long, and though
It feels like a second only when I conceived of this, how many years
Have passed? Many. Well, no doubt you must be going too, *adieu*, so long,
Like the Mariner's Guest let us together rise up as from an odd tale to attend
A wedding, older and if we can't be wiser, at least let us be unhurt and entertained. It
Is no matter at last at the bottom, all things bear the fruits of their endings in their seeds,
And so farewell, you need only turn the pages in your sweet time to see the likes of me again.

THIS, AT LEAST

Finishing a private deed—
The flowers planted,
The kitchen painted,
A novel read—

When nobody knows
Or knowing, underrates,
Is a power that grows
Over the object's need.

It is just, what it means:
The taut bow's attention,
The arrow of intention
 Striking its clear mark
 When so much else is dark.

ARTICLE OF FAITH

Whatever it is that makes
     The watery tapping
Drumbeats in our hearts
     Can't be stretched upon
The rack of what's measured and seen,

So on faith it must be received—
     Like the ether of the heavens,
Another planet hosting life,
     Or whatever is here, behind
Our breath, whenever we speak of the soul.

THE SCHEHERAZADE GENE

However else we must survive,
Whatever is treasured or lost,
We also hunt and gather stories.

Our days, ludicrous or pained,
Trigger that instinctual thought—
This could make an anecdote.

We embellish by our natures;
The cold meat stew of facts
Needs flame and spicy fiction.

Storytelling, neither food nor drink
Nor shelter, evolves into just
What our primal needs are for:

Like that Persian queen of wits
Who pleased a demanding king,
We tell our tales to stay alive.

JUST SO

Dogs are mostly affable,
Their antics often laughable—
    Once tamed to be led,
    They lap up our beneficence
And forgive we know not what we do.

But cats retain their feral eyes,
Of darkness they have keen surmise—
    Though taught to be fed,
    They are complicit in violence
And watch, and know the evil we can do.

RIDDLE MI

Neither nourishing nor sheltering
And made of nothing solid
Yet fashioned by everyone
Out of all things solid

Universal as the air
Both free and for the markets
It serves no purpose for survival
Yet no one wants one day without it

TRY THIS AT HOME

Bring your finest hammer
And a block of sunlight
Centered right above you,
Hit the light with a tap

In the flaw designed for
Splitting into splinters,

Glissading the air itself
On the tympana of ears
Down to the chambered heart.

THE WEIR

The first words arriving
Like a sunrise, filled
With glimmers of hope,
They lose their way
As the day percolates
Into many choices,
Then at midday doubt
Gnaws upon the heart,
Like the fox unfreezing
Under a confidence cloak,
Almost causing their way
To be abandoned, yet
A meal's sustenance
Revives them, so that
After the sun melts into
Resigned watercolors,
And before the thief of
Sleep takes off the body,
The last words yield to gravity,
Clicking shut the clasp
On the jewel box, with
Their maker relearning
That their patterns and sum
Can never explain
Or be better than
That quality of silence
On the other side of
The period that ends
The life of its long sentence.

THOUGHTS OF CLAY

Lord Kiln,
All of us little clay
Figurines are pitted and pocked,
Scarred or soiled with stains,
Some missing pieces in the making
Or lost after by rough handling—

Lord Fire,
We essence of clay
Are particles so weak and porous
To Your rough world that
None is whole, not one pure;
Even those with clean surfaces
Harbor scoria and scrapes within—

Lord Hands,
None can escape
Your accidents folded in;
We're matter made only to shatter,
Yet by the firing of our thoughts
We cannot help ourselves
From asking—
           If we little clay
figurines imbued with flaws
are in Your Image made,
should we worship such a feat?
Dare we love Imperfect You?

WHAT ARE FRIENDS FOR?

Joey Mankind, my crackpot friend,
has called collect for me again.
I bailed him out, brought him in,
cleaned him up and lay him down.
He tricked my lover to repent,
bolted my food and stole the rent—
I'll have to drag that stone again.

He made me listen to his stench,
then took my car upon a whim.
I prowl around my furnished den,
alone again with my pet sin.
At odds from being shed of him,
I lie in the dark and wait for grim
Joey Mankind to call on me again.

THIS MAN FOR LEASE

Everybody's on the make, the Prophet cried,
Decked in a sackcloth of tongues and eyes,

Selling goods and leasing worse,
Themselves, their rigged-out games!

Every hand is for the take, the Prophet barked
Beneath the tented markets and the sky;

So coerced, I grasped and bought
With the nerve currency of my pain

All the Prophet's products, and then tied
Four corners down on my good names.

A HUMAN GRAMMAR

I am rapidly moving on sidewalks and streets
And there is no help when strangers meet—
   I'm estranged and ill-fitting as anyone else.

He is haltingly walking with pulleys and wheels
And there is no cure for the pain he feels--
   He's broken and damaged as anyone else.

She is loudly complaining to what she hears,
And there is no way to keep her head clear—
   She's battered, disheartened as anyone else.

They who primp in the mirrors of their esteem,
Though haughty, are lower than they must seem—
   They're beaten and conquered as everyone else.

WOMAN IN HER BOOK

Say a woman is reading a book
the size of a loaf of bread
in which the marks she follows
that run through her head
signify an old man by a brook—

Say a refugee in a German wood
who is holding a loaf of bread
stolen from a farmer's window
and thinks, *If my hunger stops,
What can I start next?*

Say that thought is a reflex look
on the woman and her book's
oblivious relief, and yet her streets
are neither bread nor brook,
for the man or the woman's grief
runs more deep than all the words
that he may be or she can say.

BROKEN ON FORTUNE'S WHEEL

Morning like every other,
sunlight falls, sifts down upon
the crowns of the royally privileged
as equally on the heads of the least.
Potato Joe is burying buckets in a park,
patch-eyed Pirate is folding up bags,
Rachel is rinsing her hair by the river,
the Old Man's reading his Bible aloud,
Ruth is digging through a bin of trash.
Surviving is their business, as they
cadge and share their daily bread.

Ruth hears a voice against her will,
Joe pulls warmth from his bottle,
the Pirate attends to that humming
in his blood after the needle,
Rachel, in her shell of routine,
is strung on cigarettes and rants,
the Old Man reads, mutters and spits.

They never present well, these others
with their rags and odors—
their very being repels, making us
squirm or curse or shake our heads.

All are weaker than their demons,
none has begged to be born,
none is deemed to be worthy
to tie the laces or touch the hems
of most of the blessedly busy.

In the evening like all others,
rain pours upon the covers
of the tiled castle roofs
as equally as on cardboard and tarps.
Ruth and Rachel stretch on cots in shelters,
the Pirate on a bench in the park,
the Old Man beneath a concrete bridge,
Joe down a stairwell in an alley.
They deem their luck worthy
if their only achievement is having
endured to breathe for another day.

All are accounted for, except for
a common friend none has seen
all day— hidden under trees by a river,
under a blanket brown as earth
lies a man whose mother felt
the spear of pain in her side
that made her name him Jesus.
The man is hidden who lies alone,
sealed inside a dreamless sleep
from which he will never recover.

BROTHERS & SISTERS BREAK RANKS WHEN THEIR SUNLIGHT PRESSES DOWN

Along with the soft barrage of dawn,
The mad and the broken
Children of God take to the streets,

While those who own them
Swiftly take their powerful machinery past the weak,
Complaining of the riches that they eat.

OF WAR AND PEACE

By day, we gather our brigades
Sworn to do our damndest

To carve up and gouge the earth
Raze and raise our fortifications

We borrow, buy and barter
With strategy and tactics

Witness the walking wounded
And pray we don't become them

Of all the weapons we choose
None more quietly virulent
Than the ill-named legal tender

We gaze upon our mighty works
The thousand things contending
Plan tomorrow's execution
Then call it quits and good enough

By night, we make our swift retreats
Home to recuperate from battle
Celebrate our skirmishes
And calculate our losses

When all is quiet in our rooms
When there is nothing left to prove
We lay down our arms
And seal up all our senses
For the ten thousandth time again

One by one, alone we fall,
And practice to perfect
The act and meaning of surrender.

SAD CARNIVAL

Another weekday & the carnival's in town, where admission is free,
except for the price that time exacts.

The Painted Harpies and Tattooed Man are copasetic,
just so long as we don't talk.

I can't avoid Fire-breathing Demagogues & Daredevils on Wheels,
since their acts come just too close.

The Halls of Mirrors show me versions of myself,
which alternate glowing & grotesque.

I'm stopped by hawkers for Magic Booths of Merchandise,
food & trinkets gotten on the cheap,
then—*presto change-o!*— re-sold for market theft.

Though they eke their lower crust, Cardboard Robots dance
below the bar of dignity.

O, it is the antidote to fun to witness God's Children
of the Curb perform survival stunts.

I take a wrong turn home,
and have to run a market gauntlet in the open air.

Canaries sing sweetly from their cages
while their vendors laugh & gnaw on ribs.

BOSTON JUSTICE

"God's in His heaven—
All's right with the world!"
                  The hell it is!
                  Not while
Tyrell Wilson of Mission Hill,
born from an ill womb,
cursed address, blighted school,
and the worst friends back
in the narrow alley influence—
for lifting what he couldn't earn,
sits on a state-issued mattress,
head in his hands, in his black thoughts
beneath a rehab 60-watt light

                  and while
Theodore Worthington of Beacon Hill,
who suckled on silver spoons,
a sleeker of the criminal classes
at the broad boulevard of training
in electronic theft, dons a silk tie,
slips out his white dream car
to enter the thick of traffic
as one more leukemia cell
in the bloodstream of the masses.

LEVELS OF LARCENY

Don't fear the soiled man
who carries his life in bags
with a stray dog's sidelong stare.

Of course, he will lie.
Too lost to love, too hungry for hate,
he's unable to follow you home,
so his damage to you is slight—
unease on the street,
a handful of coins,
a glimpse of his hell
and nothing more.

But do fear the clean man
who carries a leather case,
with his dark suit, handshake vise
and that social baring of the teeth.

Of course, he will lie.
Though you run, slide the bolt home,
he'll reach through your neighbors
a slipping damage to you—
your fortune foundation,
a glimpse of his power
and once inside, much more.

CLOSE ENOUGH TO CHRISTMAS EVE

In the lees of a frigid day
            beneath a holly wreath
lashed to a light pole,

a man clad in plastic bags
            turning still and gray from dusk
sits cross-legged on a curb.

He holds the one word *HELP*
            scrawled on a cardboard sign,
and stares at the freezing ground.

From the crowd in the parking lot,
            another man with grayer hair
brings a bag of oranges and bread.

One stretches his arm to the other,
            who reaches out with his hand
in that ancient gesture signifying

nothing and yet most of it,
            inside a night that only knows
how to get darker and colder.

PEACE, THAT HOLDING ACTION

Wars and rumors of war
Occupy the minds of the old
And shock the flesh of the young;
Cain slew Abel, that ancient story
Told in my hands bleeding black
From today's newspaper page;
A man with a gun, an ape
With a thing in its hand,
Proved John Lennon dead wrong;
The battles on streets and in homes,
Mano a mano, surpass the count
Of soldiers massing on fronts—
   Violence, our feverish curse.

Go bare your teeth to a mirror,
Stare at your beetle-browed kin,
At those incisors and canines
All the better to eat lives with.
Lift up that grasping hand,
Flex a grip that handles things
And imagine what falls down.

This, our eternal crimson spell,
This brew that is boiling,
It's roiling, it's all spilling over
The lip of the cauldron,
 So come over here,
Lend us your hand for God's stake,
In whatever you do press down
With ours on the rattling lid—
Better to be scalded than taken
In single combat, or swept away
In the clamor for just one more war.

ACHILLES REDUX

That armored thug who cut you off
          Shall choke someday on his just deserts
              No matter how invincible he feels,
       For Danger embraces those who flirt
And Time wounds all heels.

"I AM SO BEAUTIFUL TO ME"

Forget about that ancient myth:
  Narcissus cannot die.

Plastic mirror in my hand,
  Who is more beautiful than I?

Stare into a crystal pool,
   No more can catch the eye;

Tamely bow to the liquid screen
  While the wild world whirls by.

THE DEATH OF EXCELLENCE

To be known for designing cathedrals,
For preventing or curing diseases,
For engineering stronger bridges,
For inventing efficient machines,
For discovering means to increase crops—
That is the tree of labor's fruits.

To be known for yelling in blameless anger,
For mugging to microphones and cameras,
For claiming the *status quo* as brilliant,
For inventing only comments on oneself,
For expecting greatness by showing up—
That is the tree of shallow roots.

Warhol's fifteen-minute party
Is replaced by a supplement,
An orgy of entitlement
For fifteen megabytes of fame; anyone
Who lusted to be seen has made the scene
At the Funeral for the Excellent.

The mob was filmed in its zealous chant,
"We rule, we're Number One,
No one needs to be better than us!"
As they lit and danced around
The bonfire of achievements.
Their party over, the roads are jammed.
By their deafening din they are known—
The bland leading the bored into ditches of sand.

MAN OF GLASS

That day
it was an old man bent over,
thin as the cane he leaned upon,
shuffling along a crowded sidewalk
who congealed in my head
like a gout of blood.

When others rushed close, he froze,
invisible as a pane of glass,
as though afraid if bumped
his bones would shatter on the spot.
He crept around the corner;
I can't vouch he made it home.

In my prime, I'd have been as blind
as those youth who hurried by;
in this time, it's mostly the old I notice.

I stretched in bed that night
wrapped in my wound-up sheet,
my hands folded on my chest,
and prayed as far as thoughts can reach
that whatever lies in wait for me
happens for the best, and before
I too have become a man of glass.

LINES COMPOSED ABOVE TAINTED VALLEY
much after William Wordsworth

It's for doing nothing productive,
It's for having no purpose in mind
That in riding down the west Sierra
I find myself stopped at an overlook
Of mountains and the river below.
It's ample enough just to breathe,
To be the eyes on the cedars and pines,
To be the ears for the murmuring assent
Of water rolling over elephantine stone.
Flocks of clouds shepherded by winds
Pass shadows over trembling trees.
The most I move is sitting on a rock to eat.

I feel that I think the ineffable going its way
Is quite becoming in its quietly becoming
Wind in a cobalt sky, brown trees inlaid green
And varied whites of clouds above, rapids below.
They are so overflowing with themselves,
I don't need to think. Time rolls over me
So there arrives a sense on my senses
Of a sibilant sound like wind, *peace*,
Though below that feeling I know
Beneath the hiding canopies of trees
Lives-on-lives are moving restless in their needs.

It occurs just as spontaneously,
It becomes a moment as welcome
When a young couple pulls up, stands off
At a distance respectful of strangers.
We nod, and they walk to the fence
Of the same precipice, holding hands.
I envy their young eyes and would trade my old.
I can't remove the motes from my eyes,
So everything the sun shines on is flawed.
They share a kiss, and silently they're gone.

When a frigid wind fingers at my coat,
I'm reminded this is not my place.
I ride down with a pressure in my ears;
It comes with a depression in my mind
That the slow turns in the sinuous road
Turn me melancholy, knowing the air ahead
That we've poisoned for each other
Will be mine from here on down,
And knowing the city I'll enter too well.
                              A layer
Of light, purple as a bruise, settles on homes
That I see by flickering lights; there too
Predators and prey are making their rounds.
The valley seems inviting and true,
Variegated, promising beyond belief,
Yet I know better by feeling worse—
I have for the single lock one key
That opens my hard-fought home,
In all of that shining city the one place
Where I am allowed to keep the peace.

IT MIGHT AS WELL BE TRUE
after E. A. Robinson

Three with the self-same love
stepped into a shady grove
to hunt some mourning doves.

Behind branches that wove
into a screen, a warier dove
flew into the air above,
the air that three shots clove
in twain, that would prove
to make a shock, and to move
that bird to a farther grove.

Two like a hand in glove
quickly and mightily strove
to dig an earthen stove,
and after carefully shove
debris and a stone above.

The couple, in breathless love,
emerged from the windless grove
to plot and to lie as they rove
beneath their fatal star above.

SMALL BEER
after Charles Bukowski

so i'm driving to my wife's family reunion
and i say, *i have maybe forty-five*
minutes of small talk in me.
turns out, i overshot by twenty.
no politics no art no literature
only weather doing what weather is
and agreeing to what geniuses their kids are.
i speak my quota, then slouch, quiet and glum.

then they break out the ping pong
and i straighten up
when the host announces a contest—
i spent a lot of sunless hours
in a dank game room
of my alma mater
perfecting my overhead slam
backhand slice
sneaky serve
with my odd fingering lefty grip
until I won first place
back in the Stoned Age
when *Yahoo!* was just what a winner yelled.

some skinny kid with a goatee
all smug and strutting around
limber and young
like he already owns the world
was my only match,
so i sip a cold one
study his moves from back in the shade.
it comes down to him and me.
he's quick
but I'm clever
and i keep my polite face
for my wife's sake
to keep from crowing
when I win, 21-18.

i get this two-foot trophy
of some guy running above two columns
with no plaque on it—
a yard sale hand-me-down,
yet it weighs like gold.
when we get home
i toss it in a box
and shove it in back of the garage.
my wife asks why.
i shrug, 'cause the truth of it is
i don't want it,
don't want one more thing
to show off,
but i'd be damned if *he* gets it.
i wanted him to know
and i wanted to remember
he doesn't own the world
not all of it by far
not just yet.

JOHN ASHBERY MADE ME DO IT!

The viaduct of our humors is not so prolific that
It cannot be arrested. False, false are the coats
That marriage forces. Never mind what hurts.
As quinine is a tolerance that prevents worse,
Zest in proper doses first does no harm,
But afterwards can be blamed for any fallout.

A gaunt hawk in its bare tree delivers a sky
Colored scream, yet the verve with which it
Penetrates the sensitive is comical in
Retrospect, as befitting anything human.

HAIKU BISCUITS FOR TEA TIME

Hot waterfall in
A clay cup, warm taste of earth
Into the body
*

Leaves are plucked, are dropped
To steep in water's calm
And savor of peace
*

She, preparing tea,
Takes joy from her belovéd
As he drinks her tea

AFTER THE FOOTFALL

What's in my mind that my eyes delight,
Consuming the moment as a treat
In watching a fox's relentless plight
Of nosing the earth for prey to eat?
What's in the fox's brain when it meets
Its beast of me as it runs in flight,
When fear, competing with hunger,
Wins by sensing my might?

Its watcher, a predator complete
With grasping hands and forward sight,
Wouldn't harm what's touched by light
Since others have prepared my meat,
But killers tread with ancient feet
And creatures cannot risk a fight;
So I am cast, when our paths meet,
As the Eden Stalker of their fright.

MULE

why am i made
to deserve this load,
to receive the sting
from that long thing
from this tall one?

what could i do
to those loud ones?
what have i have i done?
this i cry, *why and why and why*

to unhearing ones
in the low notes i was given

MOLE

i love that earth
hugs me warm
or cools my sides

who needs to see?

sweet worms
and sour soil

are enough, enough!

not for me
a blinding light,
not for me a heaven

it suffices to be dark
and given dirt to leaven

A MISS IS AS GOOD AS A HIT

Cool, calm and content are the calls of the ducks and geese
       Silent, warm and bright is the sun that stipples the water

  A gunmetal falcon shoots from a tower,
    Strafing a cluster of ducks that rises to scatter—
  As the falcon pivots and stoops, banking to cut off a few,
    It grasps a teal that twists to slip from the falcon's grip

  A few feathers fall, the teal tumbles back to the wheeling flock
    The falcon pulls out of its dive, planes level down to horizon,
    Dropping behind a curtain of cattails, raising a cloud of ducks
    To emerge with its dangling prey lifted to a tower strut

The sated foe, the denser pleasure of the flock,
      The forage there for the taking,
      The velvet water turning dark—
        To the victors go the spoils of truce

THE WORK OF TIDES

As I stepped past, a heaped-up gull on the surf line,
       its wings splaying a pattern on the sands,
            its head bedraggled, stared out with vacant eye.

I moved along the beach, and then felt to turn.
       A raven, standing on the gull, brought its hammer down
         upon the neck that moved up,
            then down, and then still.

What happened next, I moved away from knowing.

Retracing my trail on the surf, I saw a few white feathers
       small and pale as the foam on the rising tide
            that scoured the faceless sand.

BEAUTY AND ITS BEASTS

It is wholly in the hanging up there in the air,
        in making aslant, ragged circles with itself
that one red-tailed hawk seems to compose

a beauty more pure
        than a second, merely
                statuesque perched in an oak—

both hawks in my doubled sight
        as I stand witness by
fields finely made as moving sculpture,

but seeming is not being,
        I am reminded
when the higher one spirals, dissolving into blue

while the lower one pushes off
  and drops
      down, wings flared

the very angel of death
        onto a vole,
  and upon its rise

the slayer and the slain
        resolve to single beauty
now in this, my undivided eye.

ON A SAUNTER

I drive to where there are no voices.
  Leaving purpose back in the car,
I saunter across a wooded field.

With no intent, I arrive at an oak
  shaped like a gnarled wizard
stopped mid-stride, as if by a spell.

I consider its sap rising unbidden,
               its roots in their nutrient thirst
from no command, its leaves taking light
               without the trunk's volition; also

consider my blood in its set course,
               my body leaching nourishment
not needful of my mind's consent,
               my lungs complicit with the air.

In a sudden,
               something of its own rejoices.

I can't dream of a better thing
  than to stop here in the shade,
to stand feet still, hands at sides,
to stare long at the wizened oak
that has no will and makes no choices.

ASPEN STAND

Back in a gold-flake grove
On limbs of slender silver
Where the winds are seen
By their rattle quake of leaves,
A prehensile pulse
Makes my hand

To grip the shining
Throat of a thin trunk,
Just as a great gust shakes
That tree, and thrums
Vibration down
Along my limb,

Down the spine to earth,
Just as I shift and release—
Kept still, my thirst unslaked
Within the windless, silent
Limbs of slender silver
Back in the gold-flake grove.

MAKING SENSES OUT OF STARS

Alone on a desert stone,
I stare at the million pointed stars
set in their course in the firmament,
and I don't care.

My voice, in its own course,
vibrates in the desert air—
Jimmy crack corn, and I don't care,
my Master's gone a-way!

The furnaces of Heaven
set at ironic spans of space
freeze before my eyes.

Give me green cells growing,
show me something with a pulse,
and I'll sing the livelong day.

Put a tree beside me,
perch a bird above me,
place a snake before me,

then the stars make sense
where their Master's gone—
through the leaf,
on the wing,
in the eye.

…I BIRD?

That Ghost of Jacob Marley
dragging its chains along the floor,
scaring the life back into Scrooge—
I, too, get its heaviness.

Fastened to my legs are
chains to a toxic carriage;
my house is attached
with a forehead strap,
another around my heart,
and every hollow thing
filled up with gravity
is forged by links to my arms.

I tread, leaning forward
to gain any purchase
on the day, by hope in deeds,
towards an inscrutable line.

Given all in the above, granted
the lightness of the air,
can there be any wonder
(and often only wonder)
in looking up, that…

A NO-FAULT SPORT

Someone large emerges from the fog
with something limp in one hand
and his rifle shoulder-slung in the other,
a dripping hound at his heels.
My binoculars beat on my chest;
I nod to his nod as he passes on.
I cannot look him in the eyes.
A stranger, my brother in kind,
with force removed the unseen force
that made the pintail beautiful alive.

I know his fee buys his rightful place,
hunting is legal as its seasons
and it's none of my damn business,
but what's a feeling man *supposed* to do
with his foolish rage, but
open a fist and point a finger?

God could be blamed for creating
no level killing or playing fields—
a man's fingers, tools and brain
against a creature's instincts
set anciently, yet vulnerable.

I could condemn our violent,
vigorous thrall of tradition;
I may fault my hypocritical,
carnivorous, pitiful pelt of a self;

I'm allowed to censure that one bird
broken on Darwin's wheel of chance
by not flying swiftly enough;

but what I am all but forbidden
—if my heart is American—
is to take wrongful aim and never
blame the man who pulls the trigger.

MEANS AND MOTIVATION
For D. E.

He heard a music from the woods
that forced him off the trail and through the trees.
The source of the song kept shifting.
His feet lurched over stones and logs,
his eyes searched into webbing branches
for a wing, a lit shape, a flurry,
anything from which to feel assured.
                    What it was drew farther back
as though attuned to his every step forward.

The dusk was thickening to dark,
enough for him to feel his choices—
follow that momentum towards the lure
or revert to a wife and hearth, to what is sure.

That was how and why he stopped attending churches.

EPITAPH
after The Greek Anthology
For D.J.

Neither for golden coins of gain
Nor for brittle laurels of acclaim,

But from the scourge of Love he stirred
To find his allotted portion of words.

Once they were the best of him;
Now they are what's left of him.

LOGWISE, I'M SURE

Still and forgotten,
Covered in fungus—
  This log's dissolution is slow.

If wisdom needs rotting,
If bliss means forgetting—
        I sit with the proof it is so.

SPIRIT TO CARRIAGE

Not so light now, are we,
      As when I picked you up
And settled in for travelling?

Not so spry now, are you,
      As in your springy youth
And suppleness of going?

I should have heeded the load,
      Those shifting sags and bulges,
Those care instructions squeaking.

Come along, Old Baggage,
      Let us trundle together down
Westward down to Gravity Gulch.

THE BODY-MIND CONUNDRUM
(a porridge of a poum)

If my body is just a housing for the mind,
  It's a lousy tasker, like a rough rind
Bossing around its pulp, like an orange
  Trying to harmonize with an R flange...
            They just will not, cannot fit,
      I'm in a snit, my mind is in honeyed wit,
              But my hand gets stuck in it...STOP!

      Let me, you know, like change this course
With another simile, like beating a dead horse:
The mind's like a fool with gold and flowers
    Walled up and wailing in drafty towers...
            Ah me, oy vey, o lackaday!
            While flesh goes on its circus glutton way,
      Or maybe it needs to don a cliché...STOP!

But all is never lost, there are strings attached,
  There are no cloaks that cannot be patched—
Even a klutzy jester, yanking a random string,
      Will sometimes make Patch Puppet sing.

FRUITLESS VINE

Since the lazy way comes first,
I clipped off each leaf within reach,
and then lumbered about
for the farthest, just to return
to see fresh leaves at hand again;

Next came that effort in earnest,
for I pulled all the tendrils
to ground, so as not to offend
my clear sight, but the laden hours
pushed them up from earth again;

Then came the invasive labor
of tools and muscle to pluck
its root crowns out, which kills
kudzu, yet still more growth
damned my eyes again;

Now comes the grapple battle
for gouging my personal acre
to scorch it with flames. Though
that left a smoldering peace,
I must have swallowed a seed;

For now, at times I can't control,
when other people seem happy
or when the green world's imbedded
glory comes as waves that almost ache,
It creeps, It clings and crawls along that treachery line, always that growing Anxiety Vine.

LULLABY TO MYSELF

Lie down, Old Log-That-Walks,
Upon this loamy slab, and pray
My feverish words be forgotten,
My foolish deeds be forgiven
In the thrall of meaning well today.
Let me digest my daily bread,
The crusted crumbs of gain
With the choking loaf of loss
And never count its cost.
Let the dark dissolve my pain and joy.

Let my mind remain and my body go,
Then both rise up and engage the day
To perform for truth, and not for show,
Acts as pure as the moondrift snow.

DETHRONED DAILY

His Highness Mind thinks it's King,
Commanding its subject limbs
Invisibly swift from high behind
The glowing walls of Skull Castle—

Dig the hole, raise the stone,
Take this task to its fine end –
Come on, and stop when I say so!

But all of the groveling guts
In all of their bestial glory
Will have their ravenous way—

Stop now, sit here,
Eat this and drink that,
Come on, and satiate your glut!

Then their ruler bows down
And slumps against the dimmer wall—
A serf, a low, imprisoned thing.

NO DREAM, ONLY ME

I caught up with a tatterdemalion
 who plucked from near his ribs
a rag on which was painted
 the leering face of a beauty.

He cried, "My heart was wrung
 by the thorn-laden hands
of the Hag of Yesterdays
 who sowed it in Sorrow Field,
returning its hull to me."

Then he produced a rag of silk,
 a blank of unsoiled beauty.
"A dried husk remains of me
 for the Maiden of Tomorrows."

          And I saw upon the path
my footprints covering his,
          and I saw upon the grass
my shadow covering his,
          and I felt no surge of blood
in the limp of his wake, as on he led.

LET UP, LET GO

Whatever we grasp in the closed-in fights,
Whatever we contend to ensure our ways
       Feel no more permanent
       Than real, as insubstantial
 As the dreams that cloud our restive nights,
As the clouds that crown our restless days.

CHILDREN OF ANTAEUS, LIFTED

When I see drivers rolling in line
for their spoiling beverages,
their feet above the ground;

When I recall that a lad
J.S. Bach walked on footsore
the miles from Arnstadt to Lübeck,
drinking only water and ale
to sit at the keys of Buxtehude;

Then I mourn our unknowable loss
and remember the heavy source
where light and genius may be found.

USE AND BE UTTERLY USED

Fickle is the careless heart
        That wavers like a vane
For any wind's direction,
        Pointing it anywhere
From gusts of appetite,
        From fickle sensations,
Not holding compass steady,
        The heart set at the ready.

Distant friend, let me impart
        From years of practiced pain
This singular connection—
        A flicker is the love we share
When set beside the bright
        Radiance of greater station,
If we align with the flowing forth
        Of one another's truest North.

ONE RECIPE FOR LOVE

Pick up a handful of some
Bitter something gritty
On which we both agree,

Place it in this mortar,
Shaped for convenience
Like my heart, and pound

Thoroughly with a pestle
Uncannily like your fist,
Until we agree to endure

Its consistency, then serve
With a pinch of laughter.
This makes a meager meal,

True, but life takes less;
I harbor no finer hunger,
And you have no finer dish.

BIG FISH, SMALL POND

One's gift is not so delicious
as that phrase appears to be,
for a big fish is roundly shunned
due to its size, its accidental flaw;
though its heart may be capacious
to contain all others feelingly,
so too is its despised maw.

It would be more propitious
to find a farther ocean,
to be transfigured utterly
by monstrous water motions
and that way sing on swimmingly,
its talent dissolved in the raw
by the size-forgiving sea.

POLLY WANTS A CHAPBOOK

We popinjays are a funny lot.
Cage us in a stuffy room
and we'll parrot our praises
in a mutual preening,

yet where no one sees the blot
most think they have no peer,
their *pretty me* so overlooked
by who is near and dear;

whether for present plumage
or future colors molting,
each bird in the ruffled flock
sees itself as the next bright wings.

Be sincere as a gentle weather,
fellow fowl, be humble as a zero—
although our perches are distinct,
our owner has loaned every feather.

CIRO'S LEGACY

Peasants out of Sicily's poor soil,
Ciro and Angelina, newly wed,
Sailed to the Twentieth Century
In the steerage of a steamship
With their fellow cattle masses,
Destined for New York tenements
Designed for their kind and kin.
Their sum of wealth was in one trunk.
They lifted their eyes to the Liberty torch
And stumbled onto The Promised Land,
Knowing neither its right language
Nor its unwritten laws for the poor.

Ciro's capital was his callused hands.
He joined the droves who gladly slaved
For New York Transit, blasting rock,
Shoveling earth for subway tracks.
Ciro was a tough digging tool, working
Two shifts straight if they'd let him.
His children, future workers and
His living investments, came in succession
Until there were six daughters,
Four sons, and so Ciro dug harder,
Mining his city's treasure
Until a rock slipped, crushed his hand.
The foreman fired 'the stupid Dago'
For his bad luck, in that same hour
Replacing him with a hungry man.
Ciro's hands, even the one crippled
For lack of proper care, were still strong
For repairing the broken, installing the new
That was needed in his own brownstone.
Coming of age, his children labored
To contribute or by leaving relieve
Their family packed in a railroad flat.
Anytime, and the living wasn't easy.
Their cherished items—icebox, radio,
Bible, stove—were meager, yet enough.

Ciro and Angelina, now forever wed,
Felt lucky with their children,
But with grandchildren blessed,
And I am counted one of them.
Of all the men in that full line,

The last to carry the family name, I sail
With my wife into The Twenty-first Century
In a boat laden with the heavy freight
Of this brazen New World, where
A multitude of things comprise The Golden Calf.
Grateful for such wealth, still I wonder,
Is this the American dream, to sleep as a serf
of wages and awake as a prince of chattel?

Unlike Ciro's, my hands are soft.
I earn my keep by my wits and pen,
Digging my way through paper.
I'm protected and guarded at all points
From abuse at work, from want in age,
From lack of care if my health declines
By laws, by unions, and a government
That never heeded Ciro's needs.

Back then, this lie was colorfully told—
The streets of New York were paved with gold.
It was Ciro and his working brethren class
Who lay their bodies down to raise a city,
Their bones the truer paving stones.

I never knew the man that Ciro was.
Instead, I own some photographs,
Always with his wife, sometimes
With their children, and only
In his buttoned-up Sunday suit.
He stands erect in all, never smiling,
As though to be caught grinning
Would lack the duty of dignity.

I am twice blessed and thrice fulfilled,
In good measure due to a peasant
Who having nothing gave his all
To pave the road for those he'd never see.
Try as I might, become what I may be,
I could never achieve or even feel
That grim joy of self-sacrifice
That is a poor man's legacy.

NO FOOLING

I wish I could make more glee.
I'd gladly trade my lugubrious hand
for one out of an unstacked deck
that could make you laugh
loud enough not to cry.

Once I knew a great buffoon
I could depend upon for nothing
except being the party in a room.
Cackling the livelong day
like a drunken oaf on a haystack,
he would banter and flirt
regardless of anyone's wants,
heedless of anyone's hurt or needs.

What a character, what a card,
they'd say of him to me, who finds
life too rough to slough off with a grin.
I am the Jack of all that set me up;
what else can the son of a Joker *be*
but the father of serious punch lines?

DREAM A LITTLE DREAM OF ME

When I heard my stepbrother was dead
From a faceless voice over the phone,
That his fortune would revert to me,
I cried to that stranger my wish
That I'd give it all to have him back—
Foolish thought!

Yet during the forty years since,
I have dreamed my brother Fred alive
While asleep or awake to my senses,
And drew some comfort from his being.

With every bright day that passes,
My odds get darkly slimmer
When I will know my brother's place.

My wider intentions for these words
Have narrowed by weakness or fate
So only you, dear family and friends,
Hold my faceless voice in your hands.
Would you give all of them for me
To speak with you, to see you now?
Foolish wish!

Well, one can always dream.

LET METAPHOR CARRY THE FREIGHT

There's a photo I can see daily
when I open a door for food,
a snapshot of innocence—
at the sea, our laughing daughters
running from a wave, while Mom
frames them behind a lens,
and Dad does nothing but smile.

To make-believe is to play, as if
something cold pushed by
something overwhelming
could cause them harm
merely by touching them—
a child-sized wave, a silly game.

Adult children now, and separated
from us and from each other
by the needful play of work,
two women still easily laugh,
Mom still records as best she can—
Dad still sits upon the shore,
helpless and watchful
as those waves come rolling larger,
and with the crux of difference
in the effort needed to smile.

HARRY D. IN PURGATORY

Harry D. is sick at heart, he's ill at ease,
    although his pulpy clock runs no disease—
    sick of the stores and every chore,
    even nearly sick of templed Art.

Harry feels the streets he rides,
    noting what he's seen before,
    dotes on where he's been before;
    sick from what he knows, as well
    as what he knows not what.

Harry guesses that he's homesick
    for places he has never been,
    nostalgia for the never seen,
    a condition without a cure
    except universal one for sure.

Harry keeps his *status quo*
    traveling away from home,
    sightseeing in lands that,
    even if they shine like new,
    cannot lift that shadow to depart
    from his world-consuming heart.

HARRY D. AMONG CLOUDS

This is how Zeus of the toga Greeks
might have viewed on green plains
those mites and moving beetles,
those miniature boxes where they're hidden,
and laughed with cohorts at our fuss.
But in the Age of the Reasonable,
The Big Deal and his raucous Company
have dissolved into the atmosphere.

Now that Harry D.
can stare through glass to see ourselves
from the disarming distance of clouds,
and *myGodyourGodourGodatthehead*
has taken residence now within
molecules of box and mite and beetle,
Harry's look long down on Earth from
a plane's a plane of more illusion.

Now that Harry D.
 is set once more on stolid ground,
it is once more pointless to stare—
now that everyone is a big deal,
proportions seem safer again,
and in the minds of those he meets
lies Harry's more familiar abyss.

HARRY D. IN SELF-REPROACH

If the tongue is a type of shovel
And love is a field on the level,
Then why in the hole am I digging?

Is the after-size of its depth
Larger than the loss in covering
That wound with the same dirt,

For it just to swallow down
To a slight depression
Made fallow by my folly?

No! Tread softly in that fertile field.
The better words are those unsaid:
Keep that shovel in its shed.

HARRY D. IN HEELS OVER HEAD

Healthy Harry, lying well of being ill,
planned hooky from work to play—
The Tempest, a chunk of bread,
slabs of cheese, a bottle of beer
and boulders by a riverside
were Paradise enough for Harry D.

Harry removed his shirt to bask.
Staring down at a sandy cove,
Harry assumed his one step down
Would be on faithful ground, but Oh!

Ass above his head was Harry,
who spun so wholly upside down,
his glasses off, *The Tempest* tossed,
and his libation shattered out,
all in the blink of balance lost—
there was a moment when all was well,
then the mind went blank, the body ill.

Oh, Harry D. was bleeding sore!
He gingerly fingered his tenderized ribs,
he fumbled forward on all fours,
without glasses seeking his glasses
hidden in the hazy maze of shrubs.

Harry stumbled back to his blurry car,
and he squinted down the fuzzy road
that would lead him to his chatty doc
for a tetanus shot and a painful joke.

Oh, Harry drove there pre-dismayed,
yet grateful for this brief time
alone with his downturned head;
he maneuvered through the land
that wavered like water to his eyes,
plotting lines for something like
a bedtime tale or comedy
that betters what happens.

HARRY D. IN AND OUT OF IT

If Harry D. sits very still
In his cogitating chair
Inside the quiet shell of home,
He can feel the thought,
The world is clean and true
And nearly gets it there—

But necessity is a female cur,
so shaking back and quickly
Harry passes through the portal,
and wends his wary way
around and through the shifting maze
of shady deals and dirty tricks.

HARRY D. IN HIS LONG COMMUTATION

Harry D. prepares in private
his body for public purposes.
He seals himself in his private box
to play his unrehearsed part
in the undirected street theatre,
rolling with the public
to an office, where he practices
and pretends to
all of the public virtues.

After performing in his shift,
fleeing work for home in
a thinner tolerance for the public,
Harry's sealed in private thoughts.

> Oh, it's such an itch of anguish,
> it's such an insufficient joy
> to make his two worlds fit,
> so what role are *we* to judge
> when Harry locks his door,
> pulls down all his shades
> and plies his private vices?

HARRY D. AMONG THE WEEDS

Down upon his hands and knees
in the pose of some rummaging beast,
Harry plucks at wayward greens
for a plot to plant his ordered ones.

Since their Lord has descended again,
spiders, beetles and ants
scurry to hide from Him—
all the fecund foam in the dirt
that Harry pities only when he's close.

Harry disturbs the soil to change
one pattern set for another,
and by walking erect again leaves
abundant life to thrive beneath,
in the powerful wake of his fond neglect.

HARRY D. ON SPECTATOR STREET

A fountain in the air
           lends a festive air
until Harry takes in too

the yellow party hat
           fire plug askew
work truck at zero

and a man with one
           hand on his head
the other with a phone

a family at the flood-
           line and lined up
at parade rest:

watching, Harry's spectator sport,
           easy come, easier go
no winning and no goal—

the fountain above
           its pool below
the man's frieze of dismay

even the truck at
           its jaunty angle
combine to make

Harry's view in relief
           in the flat otherwise
asphalt stadium of sights.

HARRY D. IN HIS BONE HOUSE

When Harry D. can be left alone,
when grubby hands fall from his clothes,
Harry obtains to his attic skull
to ponder again the Imponderables:
Where Has God Gone? Where Is Man Going?
Nothing is there but pearly shapes —
        Harry is aloft,
and no wiser in the rarefied air.

When Harry wishes not to be alone,
he roams among lights and plumbing,
among shadows soaked with colors
of publically shared living rooms,
the shifting windows from his brain
and the kitchen of ample meals—
        Harry is aground,
and no better for the gritty there.

When Harry greets the dark alone
at the altar bed and pillow loaf,
he packs his will in a small black box
and treads, step by dimming step,
down to the cavernous basement
for stranger tales in black and white—
        Harry is adrift,
and no worse for traveling there.

HARRY D. AT BREAKFAST

Harry, bent from overthinking,
bows to his gritty bowl of fuel
and spreads *The Daily Fire* flat.

He has tried, but can't be callously
exempt from the heated miseries;
what others are becomes his own.

Harry murmurs, *Fear no more
the heat of the sun*, as he greets
the smiling faces of the dead.

He assembles himself into his
semblance of a moving man,
his stomach warm as a personal oven,

and exits his temperate home
to sizzle on the frying-pan world
hot enough to sear the eggs

of dreams upon its surface.
Harry, *in sotto voce*, works
in the habit of insignificance

to forestall for one more day
the feverish and the chroniclers
of his own conflagration.

HARRY D. UNDER THE LAUREL TREE

Harry's Grecian laurel in his yard
is as seasoned as his house, its tall
canopy like a crown over his home

Harry sits under the laurel tree
with nobody else but free
association—
          the first,
to remember its oblong leaves
were woven into wreaths
for the Pythian Games, for the
 sweetest poet and swiftest racer—
          the second fold,
that no one wound a wreath for him—
          the third, a twist
how few deem Harry worth a wreath

Harry tugs a few leaves down,
crushes them into his palm
and inhales their pungency

His wife from the window calls,
his daughter is on the line, so
Harry is tugged by love inside

When Harry leaves his yard,
he thinks upon his final link—
take it as they came—
a handful of oblong poems,
a home for the heart's renown,
an accidental homage laurel tree

HARRY D. IN THE NEXUS OF NIGHT

Harry D. rises from the dark bedroom
Bringing himself to his outside dark

The stars and the closer moon
The closest wind and trees and grass
From busily careering on without him
Are briefly busy with him

Though Harry hears the traffic hiss
Of the few who are doing their day
He considers of the night
Half the beasts and humans
on the planet are asleep
No finer time to trust in God
And so returns to join them

Harry settles into the dark bed
Bringing himself to his inside dark
His sleepy brain in slippery gear—

What will morning be

How will my purpose fit

How did I get this far so soon

What

OUR DEBT TO DODOS

Dodo birds had no enemies,
None at least they knew of—
A fact that visiting sailors loved
To celebrate with their clubs.

It gives us no solace to know
That those who struck the blows
Were led by Time's sure hand
Down the path of the two-legged Dodos,

For legions of brothers in their stead
Still hold that privilege in their heads;
The kinds of birds on the slippery slope
Now number to twelve hundred.

Thank God that the rest combine
Compassion with the arm of Law
To score a bright, harsh line
So those birds won't further decline.

Although we cannot expiate
Fully for the extinguishing lot,
We can surely compensate
By forcing the violent to abate,

Repaying the finest debt we owe
To gentle creatures whom we know,
To the innocent and to the kind
Who walk like two-legged Dodos.

AT NEWSPAPER ROCK
Petrified Forest

Having come into the desert
for wonder and not to know,
we are led by the trail to book-flat slabs
to scan with abstracted gaze
the petroglyphs of vanished Anasazi.
Coming loudly from behind,
a man and woman of our tribe.

"Wonder what they're trying to tell us?"
she asks, with no stake in the answer,
as if only the living mattered
and our egos were the center.
"They aren't any good, just stick figures,"
as if art needs putting in place
and judgment a type of conquest.

They left us, immersed in a thick
desert silence from which
we read without reading—
a sun pierced by an arrow,
a feather-splayed bird
and shapes that need no names—
and we left them to be, and to be gladly none the wiser.

REQUIEM FOR NEANDERTHALS

A thickset man without a name
Daubs the stone with ochre mud.
He washes off his hands
And presses the left one down on it.
Others of his clan look up and nod,
So he presses again, again.

Going over the icy plains,
The thickset man and his clan watch
As tall, thin men walk gracefully towards them.
He approaches the first of these others,
Who reaches out to clasp
And feel of his right hand.

That tight squeeze by the other made
The hole into which
The thickset ones have fallen.
Unto the very end of days,
They have earned that lesser name
Given to them by gracious, smiling men.

ODE TO THE POTATO

Nothing much, an
Apple from earth,
Humble as dirt,
It nourishes well
The perpetual poor;

Neither spicy nor
Sweet, calling no
Attention upon itself,
But ample as
A nourishing gift.

So plain in
Bowl or pot—
May we also
Be as simple,
A modest food;

May we learn
How to serve
All who deserve
The blessings of
A perpetual worth.

"THE NECK BONE'S CONNECTED TO THE HEAD BONE, OH, HEAR THE WORD OF THE LORD!"

What on this Earth can be more Miracle than
Pulleys and Levers on Calcified Rods,
Hinged Vises and Flat Wheels,
Filigree Wires,
Aqueous Lenses,
Receivers and Amplifiers,
Resonant Loudspeaker,
Valve Pump with Conductive Pipes,
Hydraulic Bellows,
A Macerating Mill,
Beaker of Acids,
Nourishment Filtration Tubes,
Toxic Removal Baffles,
Wastewater Treatment Container,
Effluent Disposal Chute,
Blood Storage Battery,
Gene-replicating Generators,
Lubrication Dispensers
all wrapped in Porous Insulators
support a three-pound Electric Control Center
that includes a Universe?

ELEGY FOR THE CURSIVE STYLE

i.

Out of all worthy laments
for the many vanishing things—
the loss of wildlife habitat,
a less reflective pace,
a diminishing civility—
a cry for the loss of the cursive style
seems minute, unworthy of the ink.

But like the azalea Emerson found
for solitary praise beside a spring,
a fine hand 'is its own excuse for being'
that grows in value with the respect
that even a minute attention brings.

ii.

Cursive is a style we can see, no less stylish for going out of style.
The letters, capital or plain, see how they flow, a kind of jaunty dance
as vowels roll so evenly along the line that measures time,
with many consonants in root beneath the line
while some aspire to the space above the line—
the flauntingly ambitious *f*, the grounded *g*, the horizontal dare of *t,*
each linked to the next, see in sentences how they run
in boxes and drawers, in letters we save in order to savor,
as though the shapes of letters make
an attractive landscape for who they are from, and what they say—
all going, going, gone to a diminutive tapping of keys,
and if you read these earlier words upon this page,
then you just might know what that land can mean.

iii.

Think what you wish of the term—
For me, the Man of Letters sits
Straight up in a 19th century pose,
In a dark suit at his desk, staring
Stiffly at the lens of futurity,
With surety that his work
Requires an utter dignity.

They were the Men of Letters—
Those wandering seekers
Melville and Whitman,
The distinguished, and the dissolute,
Hawthorne, and Poe,
Those driven dreamers,
Emerson and Thoreau.

They, and others in that range,
Wrote at a prodigious pace
All their hard-bound monuments
In distinctive cursive hands.
There they are in the archives, go
As pilgrim, seek to know in those letters
How the streams of posterity used to flow.

iv.

Is it little or nothing to note
            the loss of one more elegance?
Do we, who make something of its
            passing, grieve for just ourselves?

No, for the flourishings of thought
            are always essential to warn us
of erosion under the foundation
            of the house that seems so civilized.

BACTERIUM REX

Whenever in my pride
I need to cut me down
to the size of humility,
I reflect on things unseen
except by microscope.

No heads there for thinking ill,
no hearts for love or hate,
yet their rods and their staffs
discomfort me, and form
the very face of dread.

A subject to my body, I don't so
much fear the heat of the sun,
the wrath of my billion cousins
or their wicked implements
for my pain or their gain

as I do Bacterium Rex
or Prince Virus the Strange—
for if one conspires to colonize,
it could, swiflty as any other
cause, put an end stop
like the ink inside a period
to belittled, olden me.

THE WIDOW QUINN

Widow Quinn takes her walk again,
sporting a stick with a hump like hers,
and a sweater hanging from her arms
like Spanish moss from an old tree limb.

Widow Quinn says to those she meets,
"Going to visit my other relations,"
on the trail where it threads from her house
in, through and out of the woods again.

If you have walked with her, as I have,
you would know how silent she falls,
how she stares, over and over again,
at a squirrel or bird in a tree—

how she pries and pokes with her stick
under logs, stones, and leaf debris
to unbury a snake or toad, how
she nods and says, "Well, hello again."

She would take the low animal in
with her gaze, then cover it up again—
in view from hiding, a moment
that brings a smile to Widow Quinn.

I received news from her last friend
that Widow Quinn walked from her house
and would not return there again.
I was given her stick and sweater.

If you have walked through the woods
as I have silently, time and again,
you might respect every other
early mother of the late Widow Quinn.

A PLEA FOR WENDY TOFTMYER

"Wendy here was born with red hair,
Plump arms and legs, and freckles
Everywhere, but her worse given curse
Lies with her last name, *TOFTMYER*,
From which she cringed and blushed
From as young as she knew hatred.

Her parents commanded her to be proud
Of the Toftmyer name, proving through
A coat of arms and several family trees
Their descent from the House of Hapsburgs,
Including a Duke whose valiant sons fought
Only to perish in The Thirty Years' War.

But what child cares for history?
Wendy was a shy, sensitive third-grader
When she began to be prodded and pierced
By schoolyard taunts of *Toffeemug, Tuftmop,*
Not to mention the burger franchise jokes.

If only her name had been Smith or Jones,
What she might have accomplished, instead
Of enduring, tight-lipped and red-faced,
Her glimpses of hell through high school.
Each of us has a snapping point, and this
Poor youngster reached hers, which is why

She did the deed for which we are assembled.
Her parents would not, and their God did not,
But may each of you, members of the jury,
So different and so variously named,
Have compassion for the plight
Of our damaged Wendy Toftmyer."

CROSSMAN'S INSOMNIA

Where's the kid who could sleep so well,
              Jack Crossman stewed in bed,
That scrappy boy with cares so small
The world never scared him at all?

Where's the young man whose slumber was sound,
              Jack's words stirred his head,
That full-blooded youth who laughed when he fell
And whistled his way through Hell?

 Crossman's body twisted his sheets around
              Alone in his king-sized bed,
              Tossed upon uncouth dreams that swelled
              Until the sovereign sun made its call.

CEO Crossman, whom no one would ever cross,
              Went where his sharp nose led
              To the office he dubbed his throne,
              Where he, with business-as-typical calls,
Drained the blood from the dreams of his legions of youth.

THE ROUTINE OF NATHANIEL QUITT

In the brilliant morning promising action,
Nathaniel Quitt shuffles like clockwork
Room to room, untwisting each lock
To open each window that adds to thirteen
In the centurial house Nathaniel loves.

In the brazen afternoon with tumult of action,
Nathaniel Quitt turns in his tether of habits,
For he loves nothing more than his comforts—
His money, his home, and his set routines.

In the abated evening resigned to inaction,
Nathaniel Quitt shuffles in clockwise
Motion room to room, shuts each window
With a twist of each lock, and counts to thirteen—

Then repeats the same with each door
That adds to three, again to each window,
Then checks each lock on every door again.

Although he survived to seventy-two
And his home to one hundred and four,
Nathaniel is frightened of the thing
That has not occurred, and this
Because he imagines it well—
A violent thief by a window or door
Making an end to Nathaniel Quitt.

No one he knew ever died that way;
Not his father, who had a bad heart,
Nor *his* father, who fell from a horse,
Nor his, who suffered a battlefield wound,
Nor *his*, lost with a schooner at sea—

Yet Nathaniel continues, night upon day,
Snug in his routine of wealth and home.
But more often lately, with a sideways
Glimpse, that scowling shadow seen
By a glance from the hallway glass—
Nathaniel Quitt is hopelessly frightened by it.

I AM JAABIR NOW
(or, every sentence is a lie except this one)

I actually chose to be born in a slum.
I'm grateful that my parents were numb.
That way, I would grow up stronger.

I'm glad my fate depends on luck that is dumb.
This way, my life tastes less bitter.

I'm pleased that I squandered my talent for fun.
That way, I had something worthy to offer.

I'm fine with the man that I have become.
This way, I don't need to wonder.

I'm happy my old age has swiftly begun.
That way, I'm prepared for the after.

I have sound advice for after my race has run.
For those who plan on reincarnation,
Be sure that you choose to be born in a slum.

THE LOSS OF JENNY ENTWHISTLE

Jenny Entwhistle coveted what she saw,
    So she sacrificed much to own it.

When it finally arrived for Jenny,
She installed heavier locks, then paid
A hefty insurance, and then formed
Conversations on its value for her.

Then Jenny measured her company
Wholly by how well they understood;
Whoever was warm, or also in love with it
Bonded as friends, while whoever felt
Cool or opposed seemed enemies for her.

There was once a young man, athletic,
Funny and crazy for Jenny, but his flaw
Was in forcing Jenny to choose, so
Soon that admirer vanished for her.

Anyone speaking of red-haired Jenny
Remarked that, though she was still
Vivacious, there was something off,
That maybe it was a problem for her.

When they finally took Jenny away,
Her neighbors gathered on the street
And wondered aloud exactly how
Young Jenny Entwhistle had lost her way.

THE RISE AND THE REST OF ELOI

When my cousin Eloi was a little boy,
his parents would pat his head in praise.
"Our Eloi has a gift that will carry him
far and high," they would prophesy,
and his art teachers chimed in agreement.
To whom much is given, much is expected,
Read the sign above the mantle, so Eloi
was lavished with toys, music and books,
then proper friends down a leveled path.
When moved to by parental sway,
Eloi would trade his gift for applause,
accepting the trinkets of their esteem
that bought their rights to plant hope
in him, for more and greater work.

With the year he was deemed a man,
Eloi was changed by the shaping world—
when he could choose to work or play,
Eloi sank to tasks as in a fever;
when the time came to relax or create,
he would reach more often for his plate;
when the time was ripe for art or play,
he would drop his tools and lift a glass.
This *wunderkind* of beautiful things
perfected the art of beautiful excuses.
Steady-going, slow and secure,
Eloi settled into his tract home,
agreeable to a fine degree,
no less content than his neighbors.

After decades in their slow, steady arc,
Eloi's parents and teachers moved
to the quietest house on the hill.
I think too much in my living room
of what they'd put to my cousin Eloi.
Since they can't, I ponder if they would ask,
Wonder where our bright star is today?
Knowing Eloi, that's neither high nor far.
Did they have rights to disappointment?
Should they judge through me now
their Eloi less than even them because
despite such promise, such leveraged care,
he wouldn't pay the price of sacrifice,
and sold his birthright for the mortgaged life?

PHILOMENA, WITH FEELING

Philomena is in a mood.
 She gives it to her garden
beyond the window pane.
 The roses and the fountain,
the granite bench, even the pines
 that wall around her garden
lend to the mood she's taking.

Philomena is reflecting on
 her twin brother, long gone
where there are no flowers,
 no fountains, where trees
 are sparse in the mountains,
 her brother, who wanders on
in a desert of his making.

Philomena presses her hands
 in prayer upon the glass
for her brother to be whole; a wind
 stirs the boughs of the pines,
the roses nod, the water trembles.
 She turns to a knock on the door
and feels that old, familiar aching.

JACOB AND HIS BROTHER

Joseph was filled to the brim with himself—
There was no room for the moon,
No place left for the river,
No space there for the wind.

Jacob made an emptied shell of himself—
The river rushed into the void,
The moon rose above within,
And welcome was the wind.

"I am Joseph, I am Joseph,"
His brother would say to women and men.
"The river, the wind, the moon..."
Jacob would say to strangers and friends.
Joseph felt dust and a life's cruel winds.
Jacob felt rivers, world without end.

Joseph was gone when he was spent.
The moon and the river, the whispering wind
Alone survive to fulfill the tales
That brother Jacob remains to tell.

BAHGREM THE BUILDER

A travelling prince in passing
stopped at an odd-shaped hut.
"Bring its builder before me."
Bahgrem stood before the prince
with his head high and arms crossed.
The prince pointed at the hut.
"How and why is this built?
Explain it all to me."

"I will not," Bahgrem replied.
"A will, like a horse, can be broken."
The builder dropped his arms to his sides.
"I cannot do this." The prince replied,
"There's a cure for one who is dumb."
The poor man dropped his head.
"I should not do so." The prince laughed.
"Scruples, too, are my purview."

And so Bahgrem began, and while
he explained, the hut trembled.
The roof and walls collapsed
into piles of sand.
The prince was pleased with the rubble.
"So it is nothing, after all. But for
this trick, and for your pride
in it, you must go into exile."

And so Bahgrem began, and walked
across dunes, to a place where
rulers have left no trace.
And now Bahgrem the Builder,
loyal to his own sun,
sits in a green desert
and creates his crooked castle
one stone word beside the next.

LESS IS MOST

I needed thirty hours for each day
When I was thirty and craving more,
Bustling with multiple schemes,
With the stamina of Sisyphus
And virtually the same results,
To save the world all by myself.

Sixty minutes in each hour is fine,
Now that I'm sixty and wary of more,
For standing still and bearing witness
To the myriad acts of the cosmos play,
For speech that may transmute to song—
Simpler tasks that will suffice
For what remains of my brief day,
And from the world may save me.

ARS LONGA, VITA BREVIS EST

I am chiseling ever so carefully
The untrue words from the just;

I am polishing ever painstakingly
My mind to keep in your trust;

I am hewing the work ever heartfully;
Forgive its flaws and my quickening dust.

ABOUT AN AUTHOR

The I was born in 1947 in New York City, in a neighborhood known as South Bronx, which was demolished to build a slum. My first salvation came from attending The City College of New York, known as 'the Harvard for the proletariat.' I received an M.A. in English from California State University at Fresno, and by strange momentum also obtained an M.F.A. in Creative Writing from University of North Carolina at Greensboro.

I taught English part-time at Fresno City College while beginning to write poetry in 1975. I found artistic employment as a poet and playwright in the North Carolina Visiting Artist Program from 1980-84. I was awarded the Academy of American Poets Prize in 1985.

A modest number of my poems, stories, essays, articles, and interviews have been published in equally modest magazines, newspapers, and anthologies. I am currently retired from having taught drama, and English as a fading language, at Davis High School in Modesto, California. Four of my six plays have been produced. I also directed two dozen productions at the high school, which comprise a shining hour. I write a monthly column on birds and birders for the Stanislaus Audubon Society newsletter.

I am living with my wife Barbara happily ever after, so far.